WHEN THE MESSENGER IS HOT

Laura Eason

adapted from the book of short stories by
Elizabeth Crane

BROADWAY PLAY PUBLISHING INC
224 E 62nd St, NY, NY 10065
www.broadwayplaypub.com
info@broadwayplaypub.com

WHEN THE MESSENGER IS HOT
© Copyright 2007 by Laura Eason

For all rights please contact Morgan Jenness, Abrams Artists Agency, 275 7th Ave, 26th fl, NY NY 10001, 646 461-9325..

1st printing: Oct 2007; 2nd printing Apr 2011
I S B N: 978-0-88145-366-9

Book design: Marie Donovan
Word processing: Microsoft Word
Typographic controls: Ventura Publisher
Typeface: Palatino
Printed and bound in the U S A

WHEN THE MESSENGER IS HOT was developed and first presented by Steppenwolf Theater Company, Chicago IL (Martha Lavey, Artistic Director; David Hawkanson, Executive Director) as part of their First Look Repertory of New Work, (Edward Sobel, Program Director) in August, 2007. The cast and creative contributor were as follows:

JOSIE 1 . . . . Kate Arrington
JOSIE 2 . . . . Lauren Katz
JOSIE 3 . . . . Amy Warren
MOM . . . . Marilyn Dodds Frank
MAN . . . . Coburn Goss

Director . . . . Jessica Thebus
Set design . . . . Marcus Stephens
Lighting design . . . . J R Lederle
Costume design . . . . Debbie Baer
Sound design . . . . Gregor Mortis
Production stage manager . . . . Lauren Hickman
Dramaturg . . . . Heidi Coleman

The New York Premiere of the Steppenwolf production opened at 59E59 Theater (Elysabeth Kleinhans, Artistic Director) on 7 October 2007. The cast and creative contributors were the same, with the following exceptions:

MOM . . . . Molly Regan

Production stage manager . . . . Jenny Deady

CHARACTERS & SETTING

JOSIE 1, *our protagonist, thirties-early forties.*
JOSIE 2, *our protagonist, thirties-early forties.*
JOSIE 3, *our protagonist, thirties-early forties.*
MOM, JOSIEs MOM, *fifties-sixties*
MAN, *plays* WASHED-UP MOVIE STAR, HAYES, CONNOR, STEVEN, BARTENDER, *and* NEW YORK GUY *and voices the* MINISTER *from offstage, thirties*

Time: The present.

Location: New York, Chicago, North Dakota and JOSIE's *mind.*

Set: should be open and flexible with the ability to change locations almost instantly. Scenes should be set as minimally and suggestively as possible to allow fluid and quick transitions.

Costumes: should be contemporary but not trendy with the same ability to move fluidly through time and space. JOSIE 1, JOSIE 2 *and* JOSIE 3 *should have something that clearly and immediately tells the audience they are the same person.*

Performance note: The three JOSIEs *are able to see and hear each other at all times, but, for the most part, the* JOSIE *"in scene" is the only one seen by the other characters. Much of the story is told directly to the audience.*

to Betsy and Jessica
with love and thanks

(Center stage we find JOSIE 1. *To her right is* JOSIE 2. *To her left is* JOSIE 3. *They are dressed in a way that indicates they are the same person.)*

JOSIE 1: Naturally, there are people who think I need counseling.

JOSIE 2: They tell me I'm in denial. They tell me to join a support group.

JOSIE 3: They suggest meditation. Or medication.

JOSIE 2: 'It's been three years since your mother died' they say, 'it might be time to let go'.

JOSIE 1: See, people think my Mom died three years ago...

JOSIE 2: And even though I was at the hospital when it happened...

JOSIE 3: I just wasn't convinced that it would stick.

JOSIE 1: My mother was too young.

JOSIE 2: And too beautiful.

JOSIE 3: Not that young, beautiful people don't die, but she didn't look sick at all.

JOSIE 2: And it happened way too fast.

JOSIE 1: My family and friends, they grieved, they sobbed, they prayed, went to groups, went to church, and for a little while, I tried that, too.

JOSIE 2: I read that Kubler-Ross book...

JOSIE 3: Denial, anger, bargaining, depression, acceptance...

JOSIE 1: But when I walked through the stages, I realized I was totally free of any traditional Mom-dies-people-get-upset type symptoms.

JOSIE 2: I wasn't in denial because I knew that her death was just a big mistake that would eventually be straightened out.

JOSIE 3: I was a little angry, but that was just because it was taking her so long to reappear...

JOSIE 2: And I would have done some bargaining around her reappearance if I only knew who was in charge...

JOSIE 1: But I was not depressed because by the time I finished that book, I knew with absolute certainty that sooner or later, my mother would be back.

JOSIE 3: And as it turned out...

JOSIE 2: I was right.

JOSIE 1: Mom came back.

(MOM *emerges holding a phone receiver and her Year-at-a-Glance book—a tattered calender/address book combo crammed with assorted scraps of paper, unpaid bills, etc—held together with a rubber band and a size 10 clamp. The sound of a phone ringing. All the* JOSIEs *answer individual cell phones.)*

JOSIE 1/JOSIE 2/JOSIE 3: Hello?

MOM: Hi, Sweetheart, it's me.

JOSIE 1/JOSIE 2/JOSIE 3: Mom?

JOSIE 2: Where have you been?

JOSIE 3: Where are you?

MOM: I'm at a bus Depot near Minot, North Dakota.

JOSIE 1/JOSIE 2/JOSIE 3: North Dakota?!

JOSIE 2: How did you get there?

MOM: There's a tunnel system.

JOSIE 3: What do you mean—a tunnel system?

MOM: There's a tunnel system underground that shuttles people out of graveyards when mistakes like these are made.

JOSIE 1/JOSIE 2/JOSIE 3: *(To each other)* I knew it!

MOM: It sends you to this bus depot here in North Dakota—

JOSIE 1: Why North Dakota?

MOM: Beats me.

JOSIE 3: Well, what happened?

JOSIE 2: Why haven't you come home?

MOM: They said there were unavoidable delays. Weather problems. Engine problems. Traffic problems...

JOSIE 1/JOSIE 2/JOSIE 3: For THREE years?

MOM: Tell me about it. Finally they admitted there was a mix-up with my ticket.

JOSIE 3: Your ticket?

MOM: I only had a one-way. When you get here you're supposed to get a ticket back to wherever you came from but there was a mix-up. Now it's finally worked out and I'll be home soon.

JOSIE 2: And, you're alright?

MOM: I suppose...the fuckers fed me coffee out of a vending machine and those nasty cheese crackers for three years.

JOSIE 3: Mom, you love those nasty cheese crackers.

MOM: You try living on them for three years. It's not nutritious.

JOSIE 1: When will you be here?

MOM: I'm on the next bus. Shouldn't be more than a few days 'til I'm home in New York.

JOSIE 3: Can you come see me in Chicago first?

JOSIE 1: There are some things I need to tell you about Dad...

JOSIE 2: And the house...

JOSIE 3: And the dog.

MOM: Is Doggie O K?

JOSIE 2: He's fine, but I think it'll be easier if you stop here first.

MOM: It'll mean I have to change the ticket. But, O K.

JOSIE 1/JOSIE 2/JOSIE 3: I can't wait to see you, Mom.

MOM: I know, sweetheart, me, too.

JOSIE 1: I'm just so relieved, you know? Because everyone was convinced that you were—

(JOSIE *realizes* MOM *has hung up.*)

JOSIE 1: Oh...O K. See you soon!

(*The* JOSIEs *hang up.*)

JOSIE 1: It's important, you see, her coming back. For the obvious, reasons, of course, but also because when she first got sick, a year before she died, I somehow failed to understand, upon hearing the words...

JOSIE 3: Cancer

JOSIE 2: And lung...

JOSIE 1: That it might not turn out well.

JOSIE 2: I was just about to move to Chicago when we got the news.

JOSIE 1: I never felt much at home in New York even though I'd lived there my whole life.

JOSIE 3: And living so close to where I grew up somehow made me feel like I wasn't moving forward.

JOSIE 2: And New York didn't seem big enough anymore for both Mom and me...

JOSIE 1: Which, I guess, says a lot.

JOSIE 3: On a trip to Chicago, I somehow knew that it was where I was meant to be.

JOSIE 2: Ater we got the news that she was sick... I wasn't sure if I should still go.

(MOM *enters from offstage. A hospital image forms with* MOM. JOSIE 1 *is in scene.*)

JOSIE 1: But when we gathered at the hospital, me, Mom and Dad...

(JOSIE 3 *becomes the doctor in scene.*)

JOSIE 3: The doctor said, "You're expected to have a full recovery! Most people in your condition—"

MOM: Well, I am not most people! (*To* JOSIE 1) See, I'm *fine.*

JOSIE 2: And I believe her.

JOSIE 1: You don't want me to stay in New York for a while?

MOM: No, I'm *fine.* We have a plan to pack you up and drive you out to Chicago and that's what we're going to do.

JOSIE 1: O K, great!

MOM: And I'm still giving the recital at the end of the month. I'm not cancelling.

(The hospital scene dissolves.)

JOSIE 3: Now, my Mother was already an opera singer, so it wasn't like the old "doctor-will-I-ever-play-the-piano" kind of situation...

JOSIE 2: Still, someone with a lung problem singing, you know, opera is not only impressive...

JOSIE 3: But a fine tool for furthering one's denial.

JOSIE 1: Which it did.

(A moment of MOM standing in the center singing an aria [or a recording plays] and the three JOSIEs look on. It should be very beautiful. This concludes suddenly.)

JOSIE 1: So, after the concert, Mom and I packed up all my stuff and headed for Chicago.

JOSIE 2: This was the most concentrated amount of time I had spent with her since I was really little.

JOSIE 3: What with her traveling and needing to be alone in her room to *rest her voice*, I didn't see her much.

JOSIE 2: Secretly, I liked when she was gone, because it was quiet.

JOSIE 3: When she was around there was always some sort of drama going on.

(MOM enters and has a moment of drama—perhaps she drops something.)

MOM: God-damn it!

(A "truck" is formed— JOSIE 1, in scene, sits in the passenger seat, MOM in the driver's seat, JOSIE 2 and JOSIE 3 are in the backseat.)

(Although MOM *can't see them,* JOSIE 2 *and* JOSIE 3 *are actively engaged in what's happening through-out the scene, even when not speaking.)*

JOSIE 1: And driving a gigantic yellow truck across the country was no exception.

(The sound of a car honking and MOM *swerves. All the* JOSIEs *cling to their seats in terror.*

MOM: *(Flipping off the driver)* Asshole.

JOSIE 3: *(Overlapping)* Oh my God!

JOSIE 2: *(Overlapping)* Why is she driving?

JOSIE 3: *(Overlapping, to* JOSIE 1*)* Why did you let her drive?

JOSIE 1: Are you sure you're O K to drive the truck?

MOM: I'm fine, it's just the visibility is a little...

(More honking and swerving)

MOM: *(Flipping off the driver)* Fucko!

JOSIE 2: *(Overlapping)* Oh my God!

JOSIE 3: *(Overlapping)* Stop her!!

JOSIE 1: Why don't I take over, Mom.

MOM: I'm *fine.*

JOSIE 1: I want to. Please.

MOM: Well, if you insist.

*(*JOSIE 1 *and* MOM *switch places.)*

JOSIE 2: Thank you.

JOSIE 3: O K.

*(*MOM *settles into the passenger seat, looking at* JOSIE.*)*

MOM: I know why you're going to Chicago.

JOSIE 3: No, you don't.

JOSIE 1: You do?

JOSIE 3: What the hell is she talking about?

JOSIE 2: Shhhh.

MOM: It's for the actor.

JOSIE 3: *(Laughing, shaking her head)* Oh my God!

JOSIE 2: She is not serious!

JOSIE 1: Mom....?

JOSIE 3: She was referring to an actor I dated in New York more than ten years ago...

JOSIE 2: Who, at the time, was almost twenty years older than me.

(Our man emerges as WASHED-UP MOVIE STAR. *He wears sunglasses.)*

WASHED-UP MOVIE STAR: Hey, sexy.

(JOSIE 2, *in scene with* WASHED-UP MOVIE STAR, *and* JOSIE 3 *cross to him and tell the story.)*

JOSIE 3: O K. This relationship was the worst among the mostly very bad relationships I've had. He was a sort of minor movie star, well past his prime.

WASHED-UP MOVIE STAR: You smell great.

JOSIE 2: I met him when I was working at a talent agency. I couldn't help but talk to him, since it was my job.

WASHED-UP MOVIE STAR: Are you a model?

JOSIE 2: Uh, no. He came into the office all the time and asked me out constantly.

WASHED-UP MOVIE STAR: Wanna go out?

JOSIE 2: No, thanks.

JOSIE 3: I knew he was your basic abusive/angry/ stalker kind of guy because he'd been on the front page of the *Daily News* for hitting his ex-wife.

JOSIE 2: And it's not like I didn't take that into consideration. I put him off for a long time.

WASHED-UP MOVIE STAR: Wanna go out?

JOSIE 2: No, thanks. But one day in a rush to pee and to get him off my back....

WASHED-UP MOVIE STAR: Wanna go to a movie?

JOSIE 2: *(Quickly)* O K!

JOSIE 3: And it would have been fine, except, afterwards, he took me to this Texas kind of place I actually liked...

(WASHED-UP MOVIE STAR *pulls out a chicken leg and eats it with much finger-licking.*)

JOSIE 2: And I didn't so much mind that he was eating with his hands—

JOSIE 3: But he had ordered fried chicken and it was like his napkin wasn't even there and he kept saying things that made it pretty clear that he was an alcoholic with an abusive past and was probably also a pathological liar with at least one diagnosable mental problem.

WASHED-UP MOVIE STAR: Cars. There are too many cars on the street. I can't live like this anymore!!

JOSIE 2: But somehow I couldn't shake him for almost a year.

JOSIE 3: Eventually he went to Chicago to do a movie.

(JOSIE 3 *sends* WASHED-UP MOVIE STAR *out.*)

JOSIE 3: And didn't come back.

(JOSIE 2 *and* JOSIE 3 *get back in the truck.*)

JOSIE 1: Mom, I told you, he was a horrible, insane, deranged, alcoholic. The last time I saw him was years ago.

MOM: What do you think you did wrong?

JOSIE 2: Oh...

JOSIE 3: Seriously...?

JOSIE 1: See, this is why I don't tell you about my relationships.

MOM: Well, I just can't help but wonder why you haven't met someone yet.

JOSIE 1: You have no idea what dating is like.

MOM: I've been single.

JOSIE 3: Yeah, like in Iowa in the nineteen-fiftiess.

JOSIE 1: It's different now, Mom.

MOM: I'm interested in you going to that workshop in Arizona I mentioned. I'll pay for it.

JOSIE 1: Thanks, Mom, but I really don't think you need to pony up two thousand bucks for me to...

JOSIE 3: Draw pictures of my angry vagina.

JOSIE 1: Draw pictures of my angry vagina.

MOM: That's not what they do. It's a very spiritual program. And your spiritual life needs some attention.

JOSIE 1: What if I'm happy with my spiritual life?

MOM: Are you?

JOSIE 2: Am I?

JOSIE 3: Whatever!

JOSIE 1: Why would you spend money like that on something I don't need but never give me money for something I do?

MOM: And what might that be?

JOSIE 2: A new computer.

JOSIE 1: A new computer.

MOM: That's too much money.

JOSIE 1: Forget it.

(JOSIE 1 *turns on the radio. A singable song comes on.*
JOSIE 1, JOSIE 2 *and* JOSIE 3 *all sing to it casually.*
It's pretty sounding.)

MOM: You should have been a singer, Josie.

JOSIE 1: You told me not to be a singer!

MOM: When did I say that?

(JOSIE 1 *turns off the radio.*)

JOSIE 1: When I was a kid. Every day.

MOM: Well, it's a nasty business. It's controlled by the gays. Or people who sleep with the gays.

JOSIE 2/JOSIE 3: Are you insane?

JOSIE 1: Are you insane? Even if that's true, you never slept with anyone to get your career.

MOM: That's why I wasn't more famous. And then there are the cunts. I wasn't a cunt.

JOSIE 2: For years, I never swore in front of my parents.

JOSIE 3: Not swearing was one of the few ways I could think of to rebel.

(*A horn honks.*)

MOM: Motherfuckers.

(*The truck scene breaks up.* JOSIE 1 *and* MOM *arrive in* JOSIE's *new apartment.*)

JOSIE 1: When we started unpacking in Chicago, I found Mom had put all kinds of things I didn't know about in the truck. *(To* MOM*)* What is all of this?

MOM: I brought you a vacuum cleaner and that little sitting chair you always liked and a frying pan since you didn't seem to have one. And I made you an afghan. *(She puts an afghan around* JOSIE 1.*)* It gets really cold here.

JOSIE 1: *(Touched)* Thanks.

(JOSIE 1 *and* MOM *hug.)*

MOM: Goodbye, Sweetheart. I hope you'll be happy here.

JOSIE 1/JOSIE 2/JOSIE 3: Thanks, Mom.

MOM: And that you'll have better luck with men in Chicago. *(She starts to leave, coughing on the way.)*

JOSIE 1: Are you O K, Mom?

MOM: I'm *fine.*

JOSIE 1: And I believe her.

*(*MOM *goes.)*

JOSIE 3: So, I start to settle in in Chicago.

JOSIE 2: And, because my Mother is *recovering* from her illness and is going to be fine...

JOSIE 3: I believe it's perfectly O K for me to go ahead and think about other things...

JOSIE 1: Specifically about *boys.*

JOSIE 2: The fact that you use the word *boys* at your age, says a lot.

JOSIE 3: But the truth is, you just find yourself more interested in men who seem like *boys*—

JOSIE 2:—ones who work in record shops or deliver things, or who sleep really late, or who smoke as soon as they wake up—

JOSIE 3: Than you are in men who seem like *men*, who work in offices, who comb their hair and wear ties, who seem *responsible.*

JOSIE 2: Even though you claim to want a boyfriend who will drive.

JOSIE 3: Who knows the exact location of his driver's license.

JOSIE 2: Who has some kind of a vehicle.

JOSIE 3: You are really only attracted to one kind of guy...

JOSIE 1/JOSIE 2/JOSIE 3: Someone who will be a bad boyfriend.

JOSIE 2: A charming...

JOSIE 3: Funny...

JOSIE 1: Exceptionally bright...

JOSIE 2: Boy/man...

JOSIE 3: Who is non-committal...

JOSIE 1: But somehow makes it seem like they are committal...

JOSIE 2: Even though it's always *really* obvious that they aren't.

JOSIE 3: At a party, I meet a cute boy who asks me out on a date.

JOSIE 1: Which is something you wouldn't do if your mother was really sick—dating or whatever—

JOSIE 3: —but since mine is making a *full recovery...* *I think, it's fine.*

(A restaurant image is formed. JOSIE 3, *in scene, is with our man, who plays* HAYES.*)*

HAYES: *(Re: the restaurant)* Wow.

JOSIE 2: HE IS TOO YOUNG.

HAYES: I like this place. Have you ever been here?

JOSIE 3: No, it looks good, though.

*(*JOSIE 3 *and* HAYES *sit at dinner.* JOSIE 1 *and* JOSIE 2 *are nearby.)*

JOSIE 1: You are Mrs Robinson...

JOSIE 2: And Gloria Vanderbilt...

JOSIE 1: And Cher in the bagel-boy phase.

JOSIE 2: He looks like he's in high school.

JOSIE 1: You'd look old in grad school.

JOSIE 2: He's only moments away from realizing that you're not cool enough for him anyway.

JOSIE 1: Even if you had been born in the eighties.

HAYES: I, uh, I read that book you mentioned.

JOSIE 3: When?

HAYES: At the party—*The Broom of the System.* I read it.

JOSIE 1: He read a book I mentioned!

JOSIE 3: You did? Just since the party?

HAYES: Yeah. I'd heard of him, David Foster Wallace, but never read anything by him...and...

JOSIE 3: *(Very curious)* Yeah...?

HAYES: I mean, WOW...

JOSIE 3: *(Dubious)* Wow?

HAYES: Wooooooooooow. I mean, it's easy to bitch about T V and what it's become to our culture, right? But

(Quietly underneath other dialogue as JOSIE 1 *talks over him)* he's exploring the super complicated relationship between the seduction of T V and the viewer.

JOSIE 1: He's saying smart things about it! He's smart and cute and nice!

HAYES: Ever since high school, *(Quietly underneath other dialogue)* I've been trying to read more, you know, "off the beaten path" kind of work...and I think he's looking at the aspects of our culture that actually effect us...

JOSIE 2: When he was born, you were a high school freshman.

JOSIE 1: When he was born, I was a high school freshman.

JOSIE 2: *(Re: pay attention)* He's still talking.

HAYES: Philosophically, even. *(Quietly underneath other dialogue)* His father taught philosophy, which was interesting to me.

JOSIE 1: I don't even understand philosophy, he's smarter than I am...

HAYES: But my roommate, John was saying—

JOSIE 3: The musician?

HAYES: No, that's Dave. John's the Actor. Anyway, John was saying *(Quietly underneath other dialogue)* that David Foster Wallace is totally under-appreciated.

JOSIE 1: He has roommates.

JOSIE 2: You have *furniture.*

HAYES: We could meet up with them later, if you want to.

JOSIE 3: Tonight?

HAYES: We'll see how we feel.

JOSIE 3: O K.

JOSIE 1: He is spontaneous. He goes out. He is schedule-free.

JOSIE 2: You take naps.

JOSIE 3: I've read everything he's written.

HAYES: *(In response to* JOSIE 3*)* Woooooooooow... *(Quietly underneath other dialogue)* You've read, like, everything, huh?

JOSIE 1: He says *wow* a lot. I wish there was a little less *wow*.

*(*JOSIE 3 *and* HAYES *stand as though dinner is done.)*

JOSIE 3: Well...

HAYES: Well...we should do this again sometime.

JOSIE 1: Maybe we should.

JOSIE 2: No, we shouldn't.

JOSIE 3: Yeah, we should.

*(*HAYES *steps in and kisses* JOSIE 3*.)*

JOSIE 2: He is too young!

*(*HAYES *steps away.)*

HAYES: Talk to you soon.

JOSIE 3: *(Happy)* O K.

JOSIE 1: *(Unsure)* O K.

JOSIE 2: *(Bad idea)* O K.

(The phone rings.)

*(*JOSIE 1 *answers the phone.* MOM *appears, phone in hand.)*

JOSIE 1: Hi, Mom.

MOM: *(Hysterical)* Doggie's gone!

JOSIE 1: What?

MOM: He's gone. The cleaning lady let him out and he's gone!

JOSIE 1: Are you sure? Have you looked everywhere?

MOM: Yes! He's lost!! Oh, Doggie!

JOSIE 1: You've told the cleaning lady eighty million times not to let him out, I'm sure she didn't—

MOM: No, you don't know that woman—

JOSIE 1: Mom, you blame everything on her when it's never her fault—

MOM: I'm not talking about missing perfume bottles, I am talking about Doggie! *(A beat, then, totally changed)* Never mind. Everything's fine.

JOSIE 1: Did you find him?

MOM: He was just asleep in the closet. Sweet little Doggie-do!

JOSIE 1: How's everything else, Mom?

MOM: *Fine.* I just wish the cocksuckers at Sloan-Kettering had told me what a bitch the radiation treatments are.

JOSIE 1: *Radiation?*

MOM: I've had to cancel all my upcoming concert dates and my agent is not pleased—

JOSIE 1: You said you were fine after the last round of chemo.

MOM: Well, what can I tell you? The idiots didn't get it all so they're doing radiation now, too.

JOSIE 1: Do you want me to come home?

JOSIE 2: You should go home.

JOSIE 1: I'm going to come home.

MOM: No, Sweetheart, I'm *fine*. I want you to get settled in there. We'll see you at Thanksgiving.

JOSIE 1: You're sure?

MOM: Have you met anyone, yet?

JOSIE 3: Well, I went to dinner—

JOSIE 1: Not really...

JOSIE 3: With this cute boy...

JOSIE 1: Nothing serious.

MOM: No one special, yet?

JOSIE 1: I've been here *three weeks*, Mom.

MOM: Well, you can tell me all about him when you're home. I have to go let Doggie out. Love you.

JOSIE 1: Love you, too, Mom. But I wish you'd let me know what's going on, O K? I worry about you and I really want to know—

(JOSIE *realizes* MOM *has hung up.*)

JOSIE 1: Oh, O K. Talk to you soon.

(HAYES *enters and another dinner date is formed with* JOSIE 3.)

JOSIE 3: That weekend, the boy and I have dinner. He is as cute as the last time, and, once again, says smart things.

JOSIE 2: Unfortunately, there is still a lot of...

HAYES: Woooooooooooow.

JOSIE 3: But not a bad second date.

(HAYES *and* JOSIE 3 *stand.*)

HAYES: This was fun.

JOSIE 3: Yeah, it was.

JOSIE 2: Don't go back to his place.

HAYES: Want to go back to my place?

JOSIE 2: No.

JOSIE 3: Sure.

(HAYES *and* JOSIE 3 *arrive at his place.*)

JOSIE 2: At his place, the art on the walls consists of band posters affixed with thumb tacks, including one of *The Police* I had when I was a kid,

(HAYES *points to the poster.*)

HAYES: That one's vintage.

(JOSIE 3 *and* HAYES *sit on a "couch".* JOSIE 1 *and* JOSIE 2 *are nearby.*)

JOSIE 2: Stay away from Pop culture but try not to get too personal.

JOSIE 3: Did you always know you were adopted?

JOSIE 2: Too personal!

HAYES: As far back as I can remember. But the thing that really, really freaks me out is that my biological mom, she was only fifteen when she had me.

(JOSIE 3 *does the math.*)

JOSIE 2: You are officially old enough to be his mother.

(JOSIE 3 *looks up at an unseen picture in a frame.*)

JOSIE 3: Is that her?

HAYES: Huh?

JOSIE 3: In the picture, is that you and your Mom?

HAYES: Uh, no, that's Anya...my ex.

JOSIE 2: *(With disdain)* Anya?

HAYES: I keep meaning to take it down, but...
is that weird?

JOSIE 2: Which part?

JOSIE 3: No. It's O K.

(HAYES *and* JOSIE 3 *kiss.*)

JOSIE 2: *(Re: the kissing)* You know, you really shouldn't.

JOSIE 3: *(Suddenly, loudly, in pain)* Ouch!!! Something is scratching me!

(JOSIE 3 *pulls out something from behind her on the couch.*)

JOSIE 3: What is this?

HAYES: It's my roommate's retainer.

JOSIE 2: Perfect.

HAYES: Sorry.

(A beat)

JOSIE 3: It's O K.

(JOSIE 3 *and* HAYES *kiss and roll to the floor.*)

JOSIE 2: Don't have sex with him. Do not have sex with him!

HAYES: You can stay if you want.

JOSIE 2: No!!

JOSIE 3: O K.

JOSIE 2: You're going to wake up in the morning without any makeup on and he is going to see your actual face! Think about that!

(JOSIE 3 *and* HAYES *arrive in a sleeping position.* JOSIE 3 *sits up and looks at a sleeping* HAYES.)

JOSIE 1: I look at him and think how lucky he is to have a mom so young, so many years away from things like *cancer* and *death*. I suddenly feel like leaving.

(The JOSIEs *try to leave quietly.)*

HAYES: *(Waking up)* Hey, are you leaving?

JOSIE 1: *(Seeing he's awake)* Shit.

JOSIE 3: Yeah, I'm sorry. I've got an early meeting.

HAYES: Wooooow. O K, well...

*(*HAYES *stands. He and* JOSIE 3 *look at each other.)*

JOSIE 3: Well, thanks.

HAYES: Yeah, sorry you have to go.

JOSIE 3: O K, well...you take care.

HAYES: You, too. *(He goes.)*

JOSIE 3: What was that?!

(The phone rings. JOSIE 1 *answers it.)*

JOSIE 1: Hi, Mom.

MOM: So, Ginny came over, you know the religious fanatic from across the street.

JOSIE 1: Yeah?

MOM: She came over saying she was worried about my eternal salvation! Telling me I'm not right with God just because I don't subscribe to her particular philosophy!

JOSIE 1: What'd you tell her?

MOM: Don't let the door hit you on the ass on the way out! *(She coughs for a moment.)*

JOSIE 1: Mom? Are you O K? Mom?

MOM: I'm *fine.*

JOSIE 1: I think I should come home.

JOSIE 2: You should go home.

MOM: We'll see you at Thanksgiving.

JOSIE 1: No, I'll come home this weekend. I'll let you know when I'm getting in, O K?

MOM: Well, if you insist. I just know you don't have a lot of money...

JOSIE 1: It's fine.

MOM: And I don't want you to have to leave your new boyfriend.

JOSIE 1: I don't have a new boyfriend.

MOM: I thought you said you met someone.

JOSIE 2: Yeah, well...

JOSIE 3: Yeah, well, it didn't work out.

JOSIE 1: It didn't work out.

MOM: What do you think you did wrong?

(MOM *and* JOSIE *end the phone call.*)

JOSIE 1: Two days later, I left Chicago for New York. When I landed, Dad told me to meet them at the hospital, which would have made me nervous except he said Mom had been practicing all morning, and sounding good, which seemed to me a pretty clear indication that this was only a temporary setback and she was going to be fine. When we gathered once again in front of the doctor, me, Mom and Dad...

(*The hospital image forms again.* JOSIE 1, *in scene, sits with* MOM, JOSIE 2 *near them.* JOSIE 3 *plays the doctor.*)

JOSIE 3: She said, if this round doesn't work she might not have much time.

JOSIE 2: What?

JOSIE 1: (*To* JOSIE 2) What?

JOSIE 2: (*To* JOSIE 1) I realize that the doctors must be completely wrong.

JOSIE 1: Right!

(The hospital scene dissolves.)

JOSIE 3: But I cancel my flight back to Chicago.

MOM: I'm hungry.

JOSIE 1: That's good. What do you want?

MOM: Taco Bell.

JOSIE 1: O K. Let's go.

(A car image forms.)

MOM: I want to drive.

JOSIE 1: Are you sure?

MOM: Yes, I want to drive.

JOSIE 2: Is this a good idea?

JOSIE 3: *(To* JOSIE 2*)* Think of how she drives—and that was *before* she was attached to an oxygen tank and on prednisone and Xanax and...

JOSIE 2: But she wants a chicken taco *really bad.* And driving makes her feel like she has some control—

JOSIE 3: But—

(All are now in the "car"— MOM *in the driver's seat,* JOSIE 1, *in scene, in the passenger seat,* JOSIE 2 *and* JOSIE 3 *in the back seat.)*

JOSIE 1: Hey, Mom...maybe you should let me drive. You know most people in—

MOM: Don't you dare say *in your condition.*

JOSIE 1: I'm not. I'm just saying, most people—

MOM: Well, I am not most people.

JOSIE 3: No kidding.

MOM: I am fine to drive. Really.

JOSIE 2: Look at the hope in her eyes!

MOM: I'm *fine.*

JOSIE 1: *O K.*

(The car lurches. They drive for a beat.)

JOSIE 1: I really like this car.

MOM: Glad to hear that.

JOSIE 2: *(To* JOSIE 3*)* What's with that tone?

JOSIE 3: Pretend you don't notice it.

JOSIE 2: *Glad to hear that?* Because it's probably going to be mine soon?

(A horn honks and MOM *swerves.)*

MOM: *(Flipping off driver)* Cocksucker.

JOSIE 1: Mom, that was the exit.

MOM: *(Giggling)* Whoops!

JOSIE 3: *(To* JOSIE 2*)* She always misses that exit.

JOSIE 2: Yes, she does!

(Another horn honking and MOM *swerves again.)*

MOM: *(Flipping off driver)* Fucko. *(Seeing where there are)* Oh, we're near the craft store. I'm going to stop and pick up some yarn for that needlepoint I'm doing.

JOSIE 1: Who's that for?

MOM: Your cousin Anna's new baby.

JOSIE 3: Little Cousin Anna has a baby? Isn't she, like, twelve?

JOSIE 2: Twenty seven.

JOSIE 3: Oh. *Still...*

*(*MOM *gets out of the car.)*

MOM: I'll be right back.

JOSIE 1: I'll come in.

MOM: *(Sharply)* I'm *fine.*

*(*MOM *goes.* JOSIE 2 *and* JOSIE 3 *talk to* JOSIE 1.*)*

JOSIE 2: You have failed as a daughter. You are thirty-eight and still single.

JOSIE 3: I guess she won't be making any needle-point anything for your baby.

JOSIE 2: If only you'd considered this sooner!

JOSIE 3: You could've gone to medical school...

JOSIE 2: Or taught children in Third World countries...

JOSIE 3: Or written an Oprah book...

JOSIE 2: Or achieved some other phenomenal thing she'd have been proud of in spite of not having children or a husband—

JOSIE 3: Or even a live-in boyfriend or lesbian life partner.

JOSIE 1: *(To other* JOSIEs*)* But I actually DID consider all of these things and didn't follow through on them, which clearly indicates my true nature as a selfish, horrible child.

*(*MOM *returns to the car.)*

MOM: Oh, we can stop at Fountain's of Wayne! I want a new Santa for the lawn.

JOSIE 1: I'm not really up for the Pre-Season Ornament Extravaganza this year, Mom.

MOM: Why?

JOSIE 1: *(After a moment)* We should get to Taco Bell.

MOM: *(Suddenly very tired)* I'm not so hungry anymore.

JOSIE 1: Are you sure?

MOM: Yes, I'm sure.

JOSIE 1: O K. Well, do you want me to drive?

MOM: *(Tired)* O K. *(After a beat)* Thank you, Sweetheart.

(The car scene fades. MOM *stays seated.)*

JOSIE 1: Maybe it was the medication or a sickness induced revelation, but I realized that all-in-all Mom and I were actually getting along pretty well.

JOSIE 3: She hadn't asked me about my romantic life since I'd been home.

JOSIE 2: She hadn't told me to brush my hair or put on some lipstick.

JOSIE 3: And she thanked me, *a lot*, for doing things for her and for staying in New York when she knew I missed Chicago.

JOSIE 1: Just before Thanksgiving, we went next door to the Forestas, and although she was really tired when we got home, I still thought going out was a good sign.

JOSIE 3: Dad went to bed and Mom and I sat up in the kitchen flipping through catalogs, like we always did.

*(*JOSIE 1 *and* MOM *talk in the "kitchen".)*

JOSIE 1: I couldn't believe Billy Foresta with that new wife, wearing a suit like a grown-up. He used to be such a trouble maker.

MOM: He was always just trying to get your attention. He was in love with you.

JOSIE 1: No, he wasn't.

MOM: He was, Josie. For years. And who could blame him.

JOSIE 1: Thanks, Mom. *(A beat)* You know, I've been wanting to tell you, for a while, how very much I appreciate everything, you know? Everything you did for me...everything you do for me.

MOM: That's nice, sweetheart.

JOSIE 3: "Nice"? I'm really trying to say something here!

JOSIE 2: Hang on.

JOSIE 1: I know it hasn't always been easy for us, you know? And we haven't always been...how we maybe would have wanted to be with each other. But these last few weeks have been good—well, hard, of course, but good because I think it shows that we can get to know each other for who we are *now*, you know, not just fall into old habits or whatever, and that it's not too late for us to be more...more— (*She looks closely at* MOM.)

JOSIE 2: She's asleep! Great!

JOSIE 3: Well, that certainly wasn't the tearful, T V movie moment of enlightenment and reconciliation I was hoping for.

(JOSIE *gently wakes* MOM.)

JOSIE 1: Come on, Mom. We should get you to bed.

MOM: Alright.

(*Transition to the next morning.* MOM *stays seated.*)

JOSIE 3: The next morning, Mom doesn't feel well.

JOSIE 2: I help her get ready while Dad talks to the doctor.

(JOSIE 1 *grabs a makeup bag and blends* MOM's *makeup.*)

JOSIE 3: She's still as beautiful as ever.

JOSIE 1: (*To* MOM) I've been blending your makeup since I was six.

JOSIE 2: I wish I were still six and she was sneaking me under the subway turnstiles...

JOSIE 3: Or letting me stay up late...

JOSIE 2: *Just this once...*

JOSIE 3: To watch Lily Tomlin, who I loved on *Laugh-in* even though I didn't get half the jokes because I was six.

JOSIE 2: Or at that cabin she rented where she thought there would be food, but there wasn't, so we had to have S'mores for dinner...

JOSIE 3: Or backstage that time at the opera at Lincoln Center when she snuck me into the dressing rooms and let me try on all the costumes...

JOSIE 2: Even though it was totally against the rules.

JOSIE 3: I wish we were still at Lincoln Center and I was six and we were pretending the Calder sculpture was a lemonade stand...

JOSIE 2: Or a hot dog stand...

JOSIE 3: Or any kind of stand.

JOSIE 2: I wonder what she was like at six...

MOM: *(Re: her makeup)* How am I?

JOSIE 1: Perfect. Where's your overnight bag, Mom?

MOM: *(Taking hits off the oxygen tank)* No, the wheelie bag is ready.

(JOSIE 2 *and* JOSIE 3 *hand items to* JOSIE 1 *who packs* MOM's *wheelie bag.)*

MOM: *(Taking hits of oxygen)* Pack the needlepoint *(Breath)* the Robin Cook book *(Breath)* Stationary. *(Breath)* My book...

JOSIE 2: You're going to the hospital, not for week in the country.

MOM: Socks. *(Breath)* Nightie. *(Breath)* Medicine.

(JOSIE 3 picks up a big Ziploc bag filled with prescription medicine.)

JOSIE 3: I recognize the one I'd care to ingest.

(JOSIE 1 zips up the wheelie bag.)

JOSIE 1: You're sure you don't want me to come?

MOM: Dad and I will be fine. Stay and watch Doggie.

JOSIE 1: O K. You're sure?

MOM: I'm *fine*. See you soon.

(JOSIE 2 and JOSIE 3 walk MOM out.)

JOSIE 1: Why didn't she ever name that dog? She always just called him "Doggie". It's like calling someone "Baby" their whole life. Which, to my knowledge, only occurred in the universe of *Dirty Dancing.*

(The phone rings. JOSIE 2 and JOSIE 3, reenter.)

(JOSIE 1 answers the phone.)

JOSIE 1: *(Into phone)* Hi Dad.

JOSIE 2: How is she?

JOSIE 1: *(To JOSIE 2, covering phone)* It's pneumonia, but with antibiotics he says she should be home in a week.

JOSIE 2: That's great!

JOSIE 3: But a week...she'll miss Thanksgiving.

JOSIE 1: *(Into phone)* Are you going to come home? Or should I come there?

JOSIE 2: You should go there.

JOSIE 1: *(To other JOSIEs)* He says visiting hours are almost over.

JOSIE 3: So, we'll both go back in the morning.

JOSIE 1: *(Into phone)* O K. You, too. *(She hangs up.)*

JOSIE 2: He's sure she's O K?

JOSIE 1: He says she's O K.

JOSIE 2: I'll see her in the morning.

JOSIE 3: I will tell her I love her when I see her.

(A hospital hallway forms.)

JOSIE 1: The next morning, Dad drops me off as he parks.

JOSIE 3: I walk down endless identical hallways with endless rooms of sad looking people sitting with dying relatives. I feel sorry for them but lucky for me that I have a mom so unlike most people that she can not only beat advanced lung cancer but look *beautiful* doing it.

JOSIE 1: When I finally get to her room, I find my Mom in a morphine-induced coma and there's a woman I've never seen before.

(JOSIE 1 is in scene with JOSIE 2 as the nurse.)

JOSIE 2: *(As the nurse)* It's just a matter of days now.

JOSIE 1: I'm sorry...*what?*

JOSIE 2: I'm sorry.

JOSIE 1: Who are you?

JOSIE 2: I'm the nurse practitioner.

JOSIE 3: Whatever the hell *that* is!

JOSIE 1: No, you must be mistaken. They said it was only pneumonia, that she'd be better in a week!

JOSIE 2: I'm sorry. There's nothing more we can do.

JOSIE 1/JOSIE 3: No, you don't understand—

JOSIE 3: This is my *mother*, I have no siblings or husband or children and I need more time, she needs more time, because things were just staring to get better between us and I'm sure over the next twenty years things will keep getting better so—

JOSIE 1: You have to wake her up—

JOSIE 2: That's not possible.

JOSIE 1: I'd like to see the *real* doctor, please—the one who told us that she's going to be fine—!

JOSIE 2: I understand you're upset. Would you like to see a grief councilor?

JOSIE 1: No, I need the real doctor to wake up my mother, so I can tell her that while the people at Memorial Sloan-Kettering *seem* perfectly pleasant and all, it is really full of quacks and liars and people with weird titles that I've never heard of before!

JOSIE 2: You have to calm down, Miss.

JOSIE 1: Somebody needs to wake up my mother right now so that I can tell her that I love her very much but she needs to snap out of it—

JOSIE 1/JOSIE 3: Because sixty-three is simply an unacceptable age for her to die.

JOSIE 1: You cocksucking bitch!

(JOSIE 3 looks to JOSIE 1.)

JOSIE 3: I realize I have just turned into my mother.

JOSIE 1: *(After a beat)* I do not understand for another twenty-four hours that this isn't a mistake. That she can not be woken up.

(The JOSIEs gather at an unseen MOM's bedside.)

JOSIE 3: Dad and I do nothing except watch her breathe...

JOSIE 2: Because that would be wrong.

JOSIE 3: I notice that the old lady in the next bed is no longer there...

JOSIE 2: I assume she died...

JOSIE 3: Until it occurs to me...

JOSIE 1: They moved her because my mother is about to die.

JOSIE 2: The nurse asks if we would like a priest to come by.

JOSIE 3: I say yes. Even though I have more than a few questions about god that to date remain unanswered.

JOSIE 2: When he arrives he tells me, "She'll soon be with Jesus".

JOSIE 3: *(Re: The priest)* Oh, really? Well, while you're here, I have some questions for you!

JOSIE 1: My Mother's own minster arrives just in time and sends the priest packing.

JOSIE 2: *(Re: The priest)* Don't let the door hit you on the ass on the way out!

JOSIE 1: As Mom's minister—who she always liked very much—prays quietly over her body, she starts to seem more relaxed somehow...

JOSIE 3: And I do not fail to recognize that maybe God is in touch with my mom, even if he's crossed me off his call sheet.

JOSIE 1: She takes her last breath.

(The scene breaks-up.)

JOSIE 1: I wait about an hour before crying.

JOSIE 2: This is followed by continuous crying.

JOSIE 3: Crying when things are funny...

JOSIE 2: Crying when people say nice things...

JOSIE 3: Followed by wondering what god was thinking....

JOSIE 2: Followed by wondering if god thinks.

JOSIE 3: I decide not to go to the funeral—

JOSIE 1: And then I go to the funeral.

(The funeral forms. The JOSIE*s sit and look to the audience as if up to the* MINISTER*. We hear the* MINISTER*'s voice, played off-stage by our man, but don't see him.)*

MINISTER: *(V O)* I know she would have been moved by the hundreds of people who came to say goodbye to her today.

JOSIE 2: *(Looking around)* There are several hundred people here.

JOSIE 3: Do I even know several hundred people?

JOSIE 1: I wonder if several hundred people will show up at my funeral.

JOSIE 3: *(To* JOSIE 1*)* Shhh.

MINISTER: *(V O)* Although we know that god is with us, it is also true that there are many things that remain mysterious. We do not know why we lose people we love too quickly to a difficult illness. How much god's hand is in the details of these things, we do not know. But we do know that the overwhelming compassion of everyone here today for the family she leaves behind is indeed a holy thing, touched by god's love.

(The funeral breaks up.)

JOSIE 1: I go back to Chicago.

JOSIE 3: I go back to work.

JOSIE 2: I can't stop crying.

JOSIE 1: I realize I am marking time in "days since".

JOSIE 1: I join a support group.

JOSIE 3: I quit the support group because it's depressing.

JOSIE 2: I feel surprised it's depressing.

JOSIE 1: I notice I am marking time in "months since".

JOSIE 2: I burst into tears when my Mom's car comes...

JOSIE 3: Even though it's a thousand times better than my K car, which doesn't even go anymore.

JOSIE 1/JOSIE 2/JOSIE 3: By the fourth month...

JOSIE 3: I note that no one's calling to check up on me anymore...

JOSIE 2: I assume this means I'm supposed to be over it even though I am certain that I will never be over it.

JOSIE 1/JOSIE 2/JOSIE 3: By month five...

JOSIE 1: I decide it's O K to wear one of her sweaters.

JOSIE 2: It still smells like her...

JOSIE 1/JOSIE 2/JOSIE 3: By month six...

JOSIE 1: I no longer cry ever week...

JOSIE 2: And I realize this can only mean I'm going to forget her altogether. Which makes me cry.

JOSIE 1/JOSIE 2/JOSIE 3: Month seven...

JOSIE 3: I go to the dermatologist again, convinced I have skin cancer. He tells me I'm fine and to stop making unnecessary appointments.

JOSIE 2: Idiot.

JOSIE 1/JOSIE 2/JOSIE 3: Month eight...

JOSIE 1: I give some of her things away and have a garage sale with the rest.

(JOSIE 1 *stands as if at a table.* JOSIE 2 *and* JOSIE 3 *play garage sale people.*)

JOSIE 3: *(As Garage Sale Woman)* How much is this unfinished needlepoint, dear?

JOSIE 1: You can have that.

JOSIE 3: Thank you, honey.

JOSIE 2: *(As Garage Sale Guy)* How much is this?

JOSIE 1: The Pot-holder? Um, I don't know...fifty cents?

JOSIE 2: How about ten?

JOSIE 1: Uh, how about a quarter?

JOSIE 2: Lady, it's a used, burnt pot-holder? How much you think you're going to get?

JOSIE 1: Forget it. It's no longer for sale.

(The garage sale scene fades.)

JOSIE 1/JOSIE 2/JOSIE 3: Month ten...I have a short story published in a really famous national magazine.

(A beat)

JOSIE 3: God couldn't be so cruel as to finally have me achieve something that would make Mom proud without her being around to see it.

JOSIE 1: The first anniversary is two days before Thanksgiving.

(The JOSIEs *confer with one another.)*

JOSIE 2: Who has a mother that dies on Thanksgiving?

JOSIE 1: Something like that can't stick, can it?

JOSIE 3: It has to be some kind of mistake, right?

JOSIE 2: Yeah, it has to be a mistake!

JOSIE 1: Of course! It's a mistake!

JOSIE 3: I think she's coming back.

JOSIE 2: Yeah, she's coming back.

JOSIE 1: Yes! She is definitely coming back! *(A beat)* I didn't think it would be fair to tell my dad. The wait would be hard and I wanted him to be surprised. So, I secretly had her magazine subscriptions forwarded to my apartment. And I took the dog.

JOSIE 2: He was becoming too much for my dad anyway, but I regretted getting rid of so much of her stuff.

JOSIE 3: I put what I had left in the guest room closet so it would be there for her when she got back.

JOSIE 1: I stopped going out.

JOSIE 3: Because dates weren't easy. I mean, how do you explain...

(JOSIE 1 *and* JOSIE 2 *as her dinner date, sit at dinner.*)

JOSIE 2: *(As dinner date)* So, your parents still live in New York?

JOSIE 1: My Dad does. And my Mom...well...a lot of my family and friends think she died a couple of years ago, but really it was just a big mistake. She's coming back any day now.

JOSIE 2: Was she missing? Was it like a kidnapping or a hiking accident...?

JOSIE 1: Oh, no. We were there at the hospital when it happened, my dad and I, and there was a funeral and everything but it was all just a big, dumb mistake. *She's coming back.* I'm just not sure when.

JOSIE 2: Well, that'll be nice for you. *(To waiter)* Check please!

(The dinner scene breaks up.)

JOSIE 3: Then, it was Valentine's Day...

JOSIE 1: And I, of course, was alone.

JOSIE 3: With no valentine...

JOSIE 1: So, when my recently single friend Connor, who lost his dad around New Years the year before and who I know has no romantic interest in me because he likes boys, calls me up and asks if I want to go have a drink...

JOSIE 2: I go.

(Our man enters as CONNOR. JOSIE 1, *in scene, sits with him. They have drinks in hand. They toast.)*

CONNOR: To friends you don't want to sleep with. *(After a sip of his drink)* My Mom and Dad used to love Valentines day. But now, for my Mom, it *sucks.*

JOSIE 1: In the same way that Father's Day now sucks for you and Mother's day now sucks for me...I propose that since Valentine's Day will eventually suck for everyone that we scrap it altogether. Let's make it about something else. How about "Friend's Day"? Because even if we lose a friend, surely have others, right?

CONNOR: Right.

JOSIE 2: I just think love type relationships should probably be avoided, you know, to prevent growing close to people who might die, or at least disappear for long periods of time with no clear indication of when they're coming back.

CONNOR: I couldn't agree with you more. *(He looks around the bar)* He's cute.

JOSIE 1: Who?

CONNOR: The bartender.

JOSIE 2: Yeah, he is.

*(*JOSIE 2 *pushes* JOSIE 1 *out of the way.*

*(*CONNOR *exits.)*

JOSIE 1: His name was Steven and he was very cute and very cool.

JOSIE 3: He was not at all the type my mother would like...

JOSIE 2: But I figured I could fit him in before she came back and disapproved.

JOSIE 1: He was too cool for me...

JOSIE 3: But he asked me out and I said yes.

(Our man enters as STEVEN. *He hands* JOSIE 2, *in scene, a beer. They sit.* JOSIE 1 *and* JOSIE 3 *are nearby.)*

JOSIE 3: We talked for a long time, until the bar was almost closed.

STEVEN: So, your parents still live in New York?

JOSIE 1: I decided to keep my Mom out of it.

JOSIE 2: My dad does. We lost my Mom a couple of years ago.

JOSIE 3: That was basically true.

STEVEN: I'm sorry.

JOSIE 2: It's O K.

JOSIE 1: She's coming back!

STEVEN: It seems like people shouldn't lose their parents until they have families of their own.

JOSIE 2: Maybe, but not everyone wants a family, kids or whatever.

STEVEN: Do you?

JOSIE 3: You're asking on the first date?

JOSIE 2: I guess it depends on who I'd have them with.

STEVEN: I very much want them...one day.

JOSIE 2: You *do*?

STEVEN: Has anyone ever asked you to marry them?

JOSIE 2: Um, no.

STEVEN: I find that astonishing.

JOSIE 1: I am totally in love.

JOSIE 2: Well, it looks like they're getting ready to close. I guess we should go.

STEVEN: You know, if you didn't point out that out, I could just stay here and talk to you forever. Forever.

JOSIE 3: I am *madly* in love.

(STEVEN *and* JOSIE 2 *stand. They kiss.*)

JOSIE 1: But I must admit, I had some trepidation, having been so used to bad boyfriends...

HAYES: Wanna come back to my place?

JOSIE 2: Sure.

(JOSIE 2 *and* STEVEN *sit on a couch, kiss, roll to the floor and end in a sleeping position—a repeat of the* HAYES/JOSIE 3 *date.*)

JOSIE 3: See, there's a certain thing about having bad boyfriends whereby it's just not that big of a disappointment if you break up.

JOSIE 1: And I had some concerns about what it would be like to break up with someone I was in such instantaneous true love with.

JOSIE 3: Somehow I managed to not sleep with him until the third date.

(JOSIE 2 *sits up.*)

JOSIE 2: He wore those kind-of long Calvin Klein underwear that looked totally sexy on him and the sex was great.

JOSIE 1: It went on like this for a month.

(STEVEN *sits up.*)

STEVEN: I like you, Josie. I'd rather be with you than just about anywhere.

(JOSIE 2 *and* STEVEN *cuddle.*)

JOSIE 1: But all I could think about was how soon he'd realize that he'd made a terrible mistake dating outside his cool habitat.

JOSIE 3: But when he kept being amazing, I thought, Mom can come home just after he proposes and she'll be welcomed with a new almost son-in-law that who, one day in the not too distant future, will be the father of my children and then she can needlepoint us something for the nursery and all our promises will be fulfilled!

JOSIE 1: Then, I started to notice things that usually I pick up psychically on the first date.

(*A car image is formed.* STEVEN *drives,* JOSIE 2 *in the passenger seat.* JOSIE 1 *and* JOSIE 3 *are close by.* STEVEN *has an orange parking ticket in his hand which he hands to* JOSIE 2.)

STEVEN: File this will you.

(JOSIE 2 *takes the ticket and puts it in the "backseat".*)

JOSIE 2: Are you ever going to pay those? There are like seven of them back there now.

STEVEN: I'm not paying. This permit parking thing is bullshit.

JOSIE 2: Aren't you afraid they'll catch you?

STEVEN: No, this car's not registered. Neither are the plates.

JOSIE 2: No...?

STEVEN: That's why I buy these junky cars. Once I get more than twenty tickets, I just abandon it and get another one. It's worked for years.

JOSIE 2: *Really?*

JOSIE 3: And you still worry about going to jail over that copy of *Old Yeller* you never returned to the Library in 1977.

STEVEN: And it's not like I have a driver's license. So, they can't catch me that way.

JOSIE 2: You don't? What if we get stopped?

STEVEN: I'm a really careful driver.

JOSIE 2: O K.

(JOSIE 1 *and* JOSIE 3 *urge* JOSIE 2 *to ask* STEVEN *something.*)

JOSIE 1: Go on.

JOSIE 3: Ask him.

JOSIE 2: I've been meaning to ask you for a while—why do you wear a wedding ring? You told me on the first date that you've never been married.

STEVEN: I was just pretty serious, you know, with Sofia, and we wore rings.

JOSIE 3: But you broke up A YEAR ago!

STEVEN: It's just kind of a reminder.

JOSIE 1: Of what?!

STEVEN: You know?

JOSIE 1: Of *Sofia*, who I'm sure was a tall, dark-haired Supermodel...

JOSIE 3: *Please....*

JOSIE 2: What happened with you two? You've never really said...

STEVEN: It just had to end, I guess. She moved back to Italy 'cause she was booking most of her modeling jobs there.

JOSIE 1: Told you!

STEVEN: Did I tell you about Wilber's paw? No? Well, Wilber was having this weird limp and I thought... *(Under* JOSIE 1's *next line)* It was his nail, which it was. When I looked at it, I thought it wouldn't be too hard to fix, you know, pretty superficial.

JOSIE 1: *(Talking over* STEVEN*)* Then there was a certain point in the relationship where I felt like the conversation was turning largely to cars and dogs...

STEVEN: *(Very pleased with himself)* So, I cut out the rotten nail from his paw and wrapped it up. It bled for a long time but I think it's totally better now.

JOSIE 3: Also, this idea that he was qualified to do some kind of home veterinary medicine disturbed me.

STEVEN: I told this guy about it at the bar last night and he was so impressed, he said he wanted to make out with me. So, we did and it was hilarious.

JOSIE 3: Is he doing this to be funny or open...

JOSIE 1: Or is it some type of cool ritual I don't understand?

STEVEN: It was nothing.

JOSIE 2: Um...I don't know if it was *nothing*...

STEVEN: What's the problem?

(The car scene fades. A dog beach forms.)

JOSIE 1: Then, one day, we went to the dog beach with his dog Wilber, who was actually my favorite of his pit bulls.

(JOSIE 2 *and* STEVEN *toss an unseen Frisbee to an unseen Wilber.)*

JOSIE 2: Good boy, Wilber!

JOSIE 1: We were tossing around a Frisbee with the dog, and it went kind of far at one point, so Wilber ran after it. But another dog took it and he and Wilber got into a big dogfight.

(STEVEN *exits off stage after Wilber. The* JOSIE*s look off after him.*

JOSIE 2: When Steven got up to them, the other dog had Wilbur's ear in his mouth, like, *off his head*. And before I knew it, Steven took out a handgun—that I can assure you I had no idea he had—and he—

(*Sound of a gunshot*)

JOSIE 2: Shot Wilbur in the head. He went down—dead.

JOSIE 3: I knew he would try and tell me it was some kind of home veterinary humanity.

JOSIE 1: I wasn't at all worried that I was in danger of being shot by my boyfriend, but I couldn't really pretend at that point that we weren't really different.

JOSIE 3: He didn't call me for a few days and when he did...

(STEVEN *reenters calling* JOSIE 2. JOSIE 2*'s phone rings and she answers it.*)

JOSIE 2: Hello?

STEVEN: Hey.

JOSIE 2: Hey. How have you been?

JOSIE 1: He didn't say one word about Wilber.

STEVEN: Great. Thanks. So, my friend Dan's having a prom party this weekend, like a seventies prom party.

STEVEN: You have to come!

(JOSIE 1 *and* JOSIE 3 *urge* JOSIE 2 *not to accept.*)

JOSIE 2: I'm not sure—

STEVEN: It won't be fun without you.

JOSIE 2: I don't know...

STEVEN: Thinking of you in a prom dress is driving me crazy.

JOSIE 2: Um—

STEVEN: *(Very sweetly)* Come on, Josie. Will you go to the prom with me?

JOSIE 2: Well—

STEVEN: *Please* go to the prom with me?

JOSIE 2: O K... Yes! I'll got to the prom with you.

STEVEN: Right on.

(STEVEN and JOSIE 2 hang up.)

JOSIE 2: And it was pretty fun, picking out a cheesy, but cute of course, light blue polyester dress which totally but accidentally went with Steven's light blue polyester tux. He borrowed his dad's car, which I thought was a creative use of humor.

(STEVEN puts a wrist corsage on JOSIE 2. Then, a fun fast-forward through their evening: they get their picture taken, they fast dance, they slow dance, they make-out.)

STEVEN: Come on, let's go to the beach and watch the sun rise.

JOSIE 2: O K.

(The beach forms. They sit watch the sunrise for a moment. Then, STEVEN takes out a crack-pipe and begins to light up.)

JOSIE 2: Uh, what are you doing?

STEVEN: You want some?

JOSIE 2: Is that a CRACK PIPE?

STEVEN: What?

JOSIE 2: What do you mean, 'what'?

STEVEN: It's no big secret, every one knows I do it.

JOSIE 2: I didn't!

STEVEN: It's not a big deal. I don't ever buy it myself, you know, I just get it from friends or whatever.

JOSIE 2: Crack?!

STEVEN: I only use it socially.

JOSIE 1: Watching the morning sun glint off his crack pipe made me realize that maybe Steven and I weren't meant to be.

(The beach scene fades and STEVEN *exits.)*

JOSIE 2: Even so, the first few weeks after we broke up I cried almost every minute of every day.

JOSIE 3: I was singly focused on trying to discover what it was that was so fully wrong with me that I could not keep a boyfriend for more than a few months, ever, even when he was a drug addict and/or insane.

JOSIE 1: I felt ruined. And I wouldn't know if anyone else has ever felt the feeling of being ruined before, but the idea is that it's not reversible, like a coffee stain on a white shirt.

JOSIE 2: A few weeks later, he visited me.

*(*STEVEN *enters and goes up to* JOSIE 2.)*

STEVEN: So, I've been going to Narcotics Anonymous and seeing you is part of my healing.

JOSIE 2: *(To other* JOSIEs*)* O K...?

STEVEN: I was so shut down about Wilber and you and everything because—and I couldn't admit it then—but I had a very bad problem with drugs, which I am finally facing now.

JOSIE 2: Uh-huh...

STEVEN: But all that bad stuff was just what it took for me to find my way back to god. See, everything happens for a reason, Josie.

JOSIE 2: I don't know. *(To other* JOSIES*)* It doesn't always feel that way.

STEVEN: That's because you don't always know the reason for the bad stuff happening.

JOSIE 2: How do you mean?

STEVEN: Well...like, if some old guy crashed his car into yours, you'd be very upset about having a crashed car, right? But maybe the old guy suddenly realizes that he should *stop driving* and this prevents him killing someone later on. That would be a good thing, but you would have no way of knowing that this good thing was the reason for your crashed car.

JOSIE 2: Yeah...?

STEVEN: All I'm saying is that maybe when something bad happens it makes something else O K.

JOSIE 2: *(After a moment)* O K.

STEVEN: Anyway, I just came to say I love you.

*(*STEVEN *leans in and kisses* JOSIE 2.*)*

JOSIE 3: WHAT!

JOSIE 1: What?

*(*JOSIE 2 *breaks away from* STEVEN.*)*

JOSIE 2: *What?*

STEVEN: You are my best friend...

JOSIE 3: Oh, no...

STEVEN: I feel like you are the only one who can really understand me. I started seeing someone...

JOSIE 3: You started to WHAT?

STEVEN: I met her in N A and—

JOSIE 1: Isn't that breaking rule number one?

JOSIE 3: Or at least rule number two, number one being 'don't do crack'!

STEVEN: And she's very much my type but she doesn't get me like you do. Josie, I really need your friendship to get through this.

JOSIE 2: Of course.

JOSIE 1: *(Overlapping with* JOSIE 3*)* You're going to get hurt worse than ever!

JOSIE 3: *(Overlapping with* JOSIE 1*)* No! No, you can't!

JOSIE 2: *(To the* JOSIE*s)* You're right. You're right. *(To* STEVEN*)* No, sorry. I can't ever see you again.

*(*JOSIE 2 *and* JOSIE 3 *take* STEVEN *offstage, calling the whole way.)*

STEVEN: Come on, Josie, I need you. Girlfriends come and go, but friends are what really matter! Friends are forever!

JOSIE 1: But then I was alone again.

*(*JOSIE 2 *and* JOSIE 3 *return.)*

JOSIE 2: More alone than I ever thought I'd be.

JOSIE 1: I just wanted someone to talk to who knew and understood me.

JOSIE 3: I missed my Mom.

JOSIE 1: I needed my Mom.

JOSIE 2: What is taking her so long?

JOSIE 3: Where is she?

JOSIE 2: Where is she?

JOSIE 1: Where is she?

(A beat. A phone rings.)

JOSIE 1: And then, she called.

(The image of JOSIE 1, JOSIE 2, JOSIE 3 *and* MOM *on the phone from the top of the show forms.)*

JOSIE 1/JOSIE 2/JOSIE 3: Hello?

MOM: Hi, Sweetheart, it's me.

JOSIE 1/JOSIE 2/JOSIE 3: Mom?

JOSIE 2: Where have you been?

JOSIE 3: Where are you?

MOM: I'm at a bus Depot near Minot, North Dakota.

JOSIE 1/JOSIE 2/JOSIE 3: North Dakota?!

JOSIE 2: How did you get there?

MOM: There's a tunnel system.

JOSIE 3: What do you mean—a tunnel system?

MOM: There's a tunnel system underground that shuttles people out of graveyards when mistakes like these are made.

JOSIE 1/JOSIE 2/JOSIE 3: *(To herself)* I knew it! *(Into phone)* When will you be here?

MOM: I'm on the next bus. Shouldn't be more than a few days 'til I'm home in New York.

JOSIE 3: Can you come see me in Chicago first?

JOSIE 1: There are some things I need to tell you about Dad...

JOSIE 2: And the house...

JOSIE 3: And the dog.

MOM: Is Doggie O K?

JOSIE 2: He's fine, but I think it'll be easier if you stop here first.

MOM: It'll mean I have to change the ticket, but O K.

JOSIE 1/JOSIE 2/JOSIE 3: I can't wait to see you, Mom.

MOM: I know, sweetheart, me, too.

JOSIE 1: I'm just so relieved, you know? Because everyone was convinced that you were—

(MOM *has hung up.*)

JOSIE 1: Oh... O K. See you soon!

(JOSIE 1 *hangs up the phone.* MOM *enters with her wheelie bag carrying her Year-at-a-Glance book.*)

MOM: Hi, Sweetheart!

JOSIE 1/JOSIE 2/JOSIE 3: Mom!

MOM: Where's my mail?

JOSIE 1: I have all your magazines, but there isn't any mail.

MOM: Why not?

JOSIE 1: You know, Mom, you understand, right, that everyone on the planet besides me thought you were dead all this time? They stopped writing.

MOM: Well, Christ, that's quite and assumption to make!

JOSIE 1: I know.

(JOSIE 1 *turns to* JOSIE 2 *and* JOSIE 3 *who urge her on.*)

JOSIE 2: *(Tell her)* Dad.

JOSIE 1: *(Breaking the news)* Mom...Dad sold the house and got remarried last year to the widow down the block.

MOM: Figures. She was always after him.

JOSIE 1: I couldn't be sure when you were coming back. Dad couldn't wait forever.

MOM: You would have.

MOM: Where's Doggie?

JOSIE 1: He's in the bedroom.

(MOM *looks off to an unseen room to an unseen Doggie.*)

MOM: Oh, Doggie! My little Doggie do! Mama missed her Doggie so much!

JOSIE 2: Hey...

JOSIE 3: I didn't get so much as a hug from her!

JOSIE 1: I thought Mom would want to stay with me for a while, but...

(MOM *grabs her wheelie bag.*)

MOM: Come on, Sweetheart, I want to get to New York and find a new place.

JOSIE 1: I went with her and we stopped by the old house. The neighbors saw us in the yard...

(JOSIE 3 *plays Neighbor Woman.*)

JOSIE 3: *(As Neighbor woman)* Oh my God!

JOSIE 1: And, of course, they were beside themselves.

(JOSIE 2 *plays Ginny the religious fanatic who sees* MOM, *falls to her knees, screams and prays.*)

JOSIE 2: *(As Ginny)* Lord have mercy!

JOSIE 1: That was Ginny the religious fanatic. We figured Ginny called the local news stations, because suddenly a half a dozen reporters showed up.

(JOSIE 2 *and* JOSIE 3 *become two reporters and rush to* MOM, *pushing* JOSIE 1 *out of the way.*)

JOSIE 2: *(As reporter)* Can we possibly have a word or two from you about your amazing return?

JOSIE 3: *(As reporter)* Yes, a few words...!

JOSIE 2: *(As reporter)* About your remarkable story!

JOSIE 1: She explained the whole thing.

MOM: Bus depot...nasty crackers...underground shuttle...terrible mix-up!

(MOM and the reporters laugh.)

MOM: And if there is any question that I was, indeed, dead as a doornail, call anyone who came to the funeral three years ago and saw me in the coffin looking pretty dead!

(MOM and the reporters laugh.)

JOSIE 1: No one seemed to have any questions about what they wanted to institutionalize ME for saying not too long before. "Bus depot, underground shuttle", sure! News of the story spread and before long, she became a celebrity.

(MOM shifts positions—she's on a radio talk show.)

MOM: Well, Larry, the whole thing is just as surprising to me as to anybody else. *(She shifts positions—she's on a T V talk show.)* The thing is, Oprah, we *all* have the possibility of a second chance...

JOSIE 1: It seemed to extend past the allotted fifteen minutes.

(JOSIE 1's phone rings.)

JOSIE 1: Hello? Oh... *(To MOM)* It's for you.

(JOSIE 1 hands the phone to MOM.)

MOM: Hello? This is. *(To JOSIE 1, covering phone)* It's N B C!! *(Back into phone)* A sitcom?! Yes, I'd love to fly out and meet with you. One second—

(MOM *snaps her fingers at* JOSIE 1 *who gives* MOM *her Year-at-a-Glance book and a pencil.*)

MOM: *(Into the phone)* Uh-huh. Uh-huh. No, the fifteenth is perfect! Thank you. *(She hangs up. To* JOSIE 1*)* Can you fucking believe it?!

JOSIE 1: So, Mom went to L A.

MOM: I'll call you, Sweetheart!

(JOSIE *stays in Chicago and* MOM *goes to L A with her wheelie bag. A T V show image is formed with* JOSIE 2, JOSIE 3, *and* MOM *in the center.*)

JOSIE 1: The show was based on her life/death/return from the bus depot. That's what they called it, actually...

JOSIE 3: *(In announcer voice) Return from the Depot!*

JOSIE 1: Featuring my Mom as herself and a little Bichon Frise as "Doggie"...

JOSIE 3: *(In announcer voice)* With Lindsay Wagner as Ginny the religious fanatic and Alyssa Milano as daughter Josie.

(MOM *talks with* JOSIE 2 *and* JOSIE 3 *as show writers.*)

JOSIE 1: I guess she never got the recognition she craved before and must of seen the show as her big chance.

MOM: Now, you know, I am an opera singer and I think it might be a fun thing to add.

JOSIE 2:	JOSIE 3:
Sounds good.	Terrific.

JOSIE 1: The show was a big hit. She was more excited about being famous than anything else. At the end of the first season, they brought in Alan Thicke for a guest spot. He fell madly in love with Mom right away.

(MOM *calls* JOSIE 1.)

JOSIE 1: Hi, Mom.

MOM: Sweetheart, I have something to tell you! Alan Thicke and I are getting married!

JOSIE 2/JOSIE 3: Getting married?!

JOSIE 1: But Mom, it's only been *three weeks*! I don't blame you for wanting to be with someone, but—

MOM: Josie, I'm in love.

JOSIE 1: O K...well, I'm happy for you. But it seems really fast.

MOM: Not to me.

JOSIE 1: *A moment)* Well, congratulations.

MOM: Thank you, Sweetheart.

JOSIE 1: Did you get my book I sent you?

MOM: I did. That was very exciting, seeing you finally published after all these years of trying.

JOSIE 1: Did you read it?

MOM: Of course, I did! I don't know where you get your sense of humor.

JOSIE 1: From Dad.

MOM: Am I going to be a character in everything you write?

JOSIE 1: If you keep giving me material.

MOM: Well, you're a good writer, Josie.

JOSIE 1: Oh...thanks, Mom.

JOSIE 3: It would have been nice if you'd told me that when I was eight. Or twelve. Or sixteen. Or thirty.

JOSIE 1: How's the show going?

MOM: Very well. Yesterday, we had... *(Giggling)* Oh, Alan, STOP!

JOSIE 1: Why is it every time you get on the phone with me, he has to—

MOM: *(Giggling uncontrollably)* I'll call you back in a little while, O K, Sweetheart! Oh, Alan!! *(She hangs up.)*

JOSIE 1: *(To* JOSIE 2 *and* JOSIE 3*)* All the time I'd been waiting for her to come back, I thought we'd get to spend more time together. I thought if she came back I'd be a better daughter. I thought she'd be a better mother. I thought, dying and coming back, it would change things, that we could finally make things right.

JOSIE 2: *(To* JOSIE 1*)* I think there are other things she's trying to make right.

JOSIE 3: *(To* JOSIE 1*)* You're just not included.

JOSIE 1: When we hadn't talked for over a month, I called her at home.

*(*JOSIE *makes a call.)*

JOSIE 1: *(Into phone)* Hi Alan, it's Josie, can I talk to my mom? *(She listens.)* It's Josie. Can I talk to my Mom, please? *(She listens.)* My mom, your wife, Mrs Thicke. *(She listens)* No, this is your *wife's daughter Josie* and I want to talk to my mom— *(She looks to the phone. Alan has hung up on her.)*

JOSIE 1: Hey! *(She dials the phone again.)*

JOSIE 1: I called her at work but the woman who answered sounded an awful lot like Mrs C from *Happy Days...*

JOSIE 3: *(As Mrs C)* I think you have the wrong number, dear.

JOSIE 1: I called Ginny the religious fanatic.

JOSIE 2: *(As Ginny)* You are messing with god's will!

JOSIE 1: I called the neighbors.

JOSIE 3: *(As Neighbor woman)* Sweetie, we thought you let this go already.

JOSIE 1: Even Connor was no help.

(Our man enters as CONNOR.)

CONNOR: Your feelings are understandable, Josie, but you have to get beyond this. People die. People get sad. You think no one else feels like you do and it isn't true.

JOSIE 1: I'm the only daughter of a somewhat strange and unusual person who died and no one could possibly know what that's like. *(She hangs up.)*

JOSIE 1: I ran to the checkout counter at the grocery store to look at the *T V Guide* and there was no listing for *Return from the Depot*! There was a big ad for a new show with Mrs. Cunningham and Alan Thicke but no mention of my mother.

JOSIE 2: It seemed pretty clear...

JOSIE 3: She was never there.

JOSIE 1: *(Fast and furious)* I know what you're thinking. You're thinking this is the part where I realize, via a simple metaphor, that my mother is not coming back, the part where I snap out of denial and realize that there will be no big reunion, that she will not send me vitamins or make me chicken soup again when I'm sick, or buy me a new teakettle when mine gets rusty...where I realize that we will never go outlet shopping again, never decorate another Christmas tree, that we will never again giggle uncontrollably about my cousin's famously cheap Christmas presents.

(JOSIE 2 and JOSIE 3 leave the stage.)

JOSIE 1: The part where I understand that she will never come to Chicago again and we will not have coffee on my porch, that she'll never get to meet Connor or Lisa or Tracy or my great new boyfriend (hypothetical) and

that they'll never get to meet her. The part where I
realize that I will never get to ask her all the questions I
want to ask her, like how you knit a popcorn stitch, like
what's the exact basil-to-oregano ratio for the perfect
marinara, like how come I have no brothers or sisters,
like what was I like as a kid or what were you like and
what was Grandma like then...and what was it that
made you so sad sometimes. The part where I realize
that I will never get to tell her that even though she was
completely crazy that I would never in a million years
want another mom, that even Mrs C would pale in
comparison. The part where I finally understand why
my mother wasn't there to help me get through my
mother's death, because it still makes perfect sense to
me that anyone would need their mom at a time like
that. *(A beat)* But it *isn't. (A beat)* It's the part where I go
to North Dakota and drive to every bus station south
of Minot with a picture of my mom.

(JOSIE *approaches unseen North Dakota people.)*

JOSIE 1: *(To unseen North Dakota person)* Excuse me,
have you seen this women? *(To unseen North Dakota
person)* Excuse me, this is a picture of my mother who
is missing, you haven't seen her, have you?

(JOSIE 1 *goes into a bar. There music playing on the jukebox.
Our man is the* BARTENDER.)

JOSIE 1: Excuse me...

BARTENDER: What can I get you?

JOSIE 1: No, thanks. *(Holding up the picture)* I'm actually
looking for this women, have you seen her? I think she
spent some time in the bus depot across the way.

(BARTENDER *looks at the picture.)*

BARTENDER: I did see a women a while back that looked
a bit like her, but I couldn't say it was an exact match.
Who is she?

JOSIE 1: My mom.

BARTENDER: She been gone a long time?

JOSIE 1: Years.

BARTENDER: The police haven't found anything?

JOSIE 1: I couldn't get the police involved, because, well, they think she'd dead.

BARTENDER: They closed the case?

JOSIE 1: Well, no, there is no case, because, technically, she *is* dead. But she *did* come back for a while—it just wasn't at ALL what I hoped it would be—and now she's gone again and I can't find her anywhere and I think she might be gone for good this time, but she just *can't be*, you know...? *(She puts away the picture)* Forget it. I know what you're thinking.

BARTENDER: *(Carefully)* I'm just thinking that's a sad story.

JOSIE 1: Oh...

BARTENDER: I'm sorry that happened to you.

JOSIE 1: Thank you.

BARTENDER: Can I get you something? On the house.

JOSIE 1: No, thanks.

(Willy Nelson's Crazy *[or something like it] comes on the jukebox.)*

BARTENDER: Dance with me?

JOSIE 1: What...?

BARTENDER: It's been slow all day and I'm tired of just standing around. You'd be doing me a favor, really.

JOSIE 1: Um, O K.

(JOSIE *and the* BARTENDER *begin to dance to the slowish music, traditional boy/girl dancing, his hand around her waist, her hand in his hand.*)

(*Over the course of a whole song—like two or three minutes—slowly, and with very little drama, they move closer to each other. Eventually,* JOSIE *starts to cry, letting go of everything, fully giving into her grief. After a good bit of this, she slowly gets it together. By the end of the song she is O K. The next song starts.* JOSIE *and the* BARTENDER *part.*)

JOSIE 1: Thank you.

(*The* BARTENDER *nods.* JOSIE *nods. The* BARTENDER *exits.*)

JOSIE 1: O K. THERE IS NO EXPLANATION FOR THIS!

 JOSIE 3 *takes center stage.* JOSIE 1 *and* JOSIE 2 *join her.*)

JOSIE 3: Not too long after, I met a guy. He was a friend of a friend. He was cute and flirted with me.

JOSIE 2: He was a *man* really, who even seemed *responsible.*

JOSIE 1: He was cool but not too cool.

JOSIE 2: And he seemed happy.

JOSIE 1: He was cute and cool and happy and Italian and from New York. And he had two new tatoos— one on each wrist.

(*Our man enters as* NEW YORK GUY. JOSIE 3, *in scene, looks at his tattoos.*)

JOSIE 3: Those are Chinese symbols, right?

NEW YORK GUY: They are.

JOSIE 3: What do they mean?

NEW YORK GUY: Child and god. See, child of god.

JOSIE 3: (*A little freaked out*) That's cool.

NEW YORK GUY: Some people get freaked out when I tell them that.

JOSIE 3: Really?

NEW YORK GUY: You know—peace, love, wisdom—all those are cool, but you say you've got god tattooed on your arm and people get nervous. And I don't want to make you nervous.

JOSIE 3: You're not.

NEW YORK GUY: 'Cause you seem great and I don't want you to think I'm one of those people who needs everyone to believe what I believe, O K?

JOSIE 3: O K. It's not that I don't *want* to believe in god, it's just that I'm a little unclear on the whole god issue. I mean, what is it? Is it here at all times? Does it have a personality? Does it have facial hair?

NEW YORK GUY: I know. I remember getting into a huge fight about it with my mom when I was a kid. It was after I saw *West Side Story* the first time—

JOSIE 3: *West Side Story?*

NEW YORK GUY: Yeah. I told her I couldn't believe in a god that would let Tony die.

JOSIE 3: Really?

NEW YORK GUY: The movie was on T V and my whole family watched it and we were all bawling, you know, at the end, when she's singing to Tony after he gets shot—it's just brutal—

JOSIE 3: Yeah, I know. It's, like, my favorite movie.

NEW YORK GUY: Seriously? 'Cause it's *my* favorite movie.

JOSIE 3: *Really?*

NEW YORK GUY: Yeah!

JOSIE 3: It is seriously my all-time favorite movie.

NEW YORK GUY: Well, I have it on D V D. You wanna come over and watch it sometime?

JOSIE 3: Sure.

NEW YORK GUY: You like fish? I could make you a nice piece of fish.

JOSIE 3: I like fish.

NEW YORK GUY: Yeah? You like salmon? I could make you a nice piece of salmon with dill sauce?

JOSIE 3: That sounds great.

NEW YORK GUY: Good. *(He exits.)*

JOSIE 1: I bring dessert and expect nothing.

JOSIE 2: What I have come to expect.

JOSIE 1: After so many *boys.*

(NEW YORK GUY *reenters, welcoming* JOSIE 3, *in scene, to his place.* JOSIE 1 *and* JOSIE 2 *follow* JOSIE 3 *in. The light is romantic, Etta James croons "At last, my love has come along...")*

NEW YORK GUY: Thanks for coming.

JOSIE 3: Thanks for having me.

JOSIE 1: There is candlelight emanating from every room. There are real flowers in the living room.

JOSIE 2: There is a table for two set with wineglasses, place-mats, more candles, *focaccia—*

JOSIE 3: *(To* NEW YORK GUY*)* You shouldn't have gone to so much trouble.

NEW YORK GUY: It wasn't trouble. I'm glad you're here.

JOSIE 1: There are pictures of babies on the refrigerator.

(JOSIE 3 *points to a picture on the fridge.)*

JOSIE 3: Who's that? She's so cute.

NEW YORK GUY: That's my god-daughter. *(Beats his chest)* That's my heart.

JOSIE 2: You will not see *West Side Story*. You will have sex with him before dinner is over.

(They sit for dinner.)

NEW YORK GUY: So, you're a writer?

JOSIE 3: I am.

NEW YORK GUY: That's amazing. I admire that so much. I write a little poetry.

JOSIE 3: You *do*?

NEW YORK GUY: I'm not Wallace Stevens but I guess there's time. I'm not fifty yet!

JOSIE 2: You will have sex with him right now.

JOSIE 1: There is a huge fish-tank filled with all kind of tropical fish.

(JOSIE 3 looks at the fish.)

JOSIE 3: They're pretty.

NEW YORK GUY: See how they're all bunched up there together? That's them sleeping.

JOSIE 3: Really?

NEW YORK GUY: Yeah, sometimes at night, I'll turn off all the lights except the tank and watch the fish sleep.

JOSIE 3: That's sweet.

JOSIE 1: In the corner is a cage with two little birds.

JOSIE 3: You have a lot of pets.

NEW YORK GUY: I like pets. Life can be lonely sometimes, you know?

JOSIE 3: Yeah, I do.

NEW YORK GUY: And having these little guys around keeping me company, they make me happy. It's nice.

JOSIE 3: It seems nice.

JOSIE 1: After dinner, we watched the movie.

(The end of West Side Story *plays.)*

NEW YORK GUY: Are you cold?

JOSIE 3: A little.

(NEW YORK GUY *gets an afghan and covers himself and* JOSIE 3. *He and* JOSIE 3 *snuggle, hold hands and watch the super sad ending of the movie.)*

JOSIE 3: Now *I* want to know how god could let Tony die. I mean, it is a good question—if god is all around us, watching us, taking care of us, then why...?

NEW YORK GUY: You know, I try to ask myself those questions and it just doesn't go anywhere. I ask, why do bad things happen, and there is no answer and I go about my day. I don't have to know. I believe I'm being taken care of. After some things that happened to me, I should be dead. So, I give props to G-O-D, you know what I'm saying? I'm a simple guy. It's cool.

JOSIE 2: I want to believe he's right.

JOSIE 1: I want to believe that something so simple could be so right, could need no further examination from me.

JOSIE 2: I wish I was a simple girl. *(Realizing)* Hey, he's not trying to have sex with me.

JOSIE 1: Is he being gentlemanly, *taking things slow?*

JOSIE 2: Does he understand he could be having sex with me right now?

JOSIE 3: *(To* NEW YORK GUY*)* Well, it's getting pretty late.

NEW YORK GUY: Yeah, I guess it is. I'll walk you to your car.

(NEW YORK GUY *walks with* JOSIE 3.)

JOSIE 1: As we walk, he notices I'm cold and puts his arm around me to keep me warm.

(NEW YORK GUY *and* JOSIE 3 *stop walking.*)

NEW YORK GUY: This was really fun.

JOSIE 3: It was. Thank you for dinner and everything.

NEW YORK GUY: It was absolutely my pleasure.

(NEW YORK GUY *gives* JOSIE 3 *a quick kiss on the lips and hugs her. Then, he gives her a Charms Blow Pop.)*

NEW YORK GUY: Good-night.

JOSIE 3: Good-night.

(NEW YORK GUY *smiles and exits.)*

JOSIE 2: That was one of the top five best dates ever.

JOSIE 1: Name the other four.

JOSIE 2: I can't.

JOSIE 3: But when I call him to say thanks, he never calls me back. *(To the other* JOSIEs*)* Why?

JOSIE 2: Maybe it wasn't a date?

JOSIE 1: Maybe he's gay.

JOSIE 3: Oh, no, it was a date.

JOSIE 2: Maybe he was intimidated?

JOSIE 3: No. He didn't seem like it.

JOSIE 1: Maybe in his mind romance doesn't have to mean romance.

JOSIE 2: Maybe he just likes candles—he is Italian.

JOSIE 3: I just keep thinking about what he said, "I don't have to know. I believe I'm being taken care of". *(Realizing)* Maybe this is the only way god knows how to reach me.

JOSIE 2: Maybe I am being taken care of.

JOSIE 1: Maybe god knows I will not pick up his messages if the messenger isn't hot.

JOSIE 3: Or maybe this was just god's way of showing me what a date should be like. *(To audience)* Either way, I stopped trying to figure it out. I let it go. I decide to let go and let god...

(JOSIE 2 *steps forward.* JOSIE 1 *hands her* MOM's *Year-at-a-glance book and* JOSIE 3 *hands her a Christmas card.*)

JOSIE 2: That Christmas for the first time ever, I sent out cards myself. Mom had always done it but someone finally took a picture of me I didn't hate and since I was wearing a red shirt I thought it would be a perfect holiday card. I put a special nondenominational greeting on there— Hey, happy holidays! I thought the *Hey* gave it a personal touch. I sent them to my friends and all the old family friends from my mother's Christmas card list. I started to get some cards back with responses like...

JOSIE 1: Good for you!

JOSIE 2: Which I *thought* was a supportive response to me getting on with my life until I got an email from someone who said...

JOSIE 3: I hope I caught you before you send out any more cards. I don't want you to embarrass yourself.

JOSIE 2: I looked at the card again to see if I was exposed in some way...or if the printers accidentally said— *Hey, Merry Christmas Bitches!* But it was just right. So, I emailed her back and said I didn't understand what she meant and she emailed back, saying...

JOSIE 3: Most people who send cards like that usually have a husband or a baby in the picture, too.

JOSIE 2: So, I emailed her back and said, well, I am not most people.

JOSIE 3: I am not most people.

JOSIE 1: I am not most people.

(A great fun, fast, loud song plays.)

(Blackout)

END OF PLAY

www.ingramcontent.com/pod-product-compliance
Lightning Source LLC
Chambersburg PA
CBHW052220090426
42741CB00010B/2610